BEHIND THE BLUE DOOR

A MAXIMALIST MANTRA

JOHN DEMSEY

WRITTEN BY ALINA CHO

PHOTOGRAPHY BY DOUGLAS FRIEDMAN

VENDOME

NEW YORK · LONDON

PIERO SAUVAGE · CASA LOPEZ · EFFORTLESS STYLE · Flammarion

wonderland   annie leibovitz

PREFACE 13
INTRODUCTION 14

ONE 20
TWO LIVING ROOM 71
LIBRARY 105
THREE 130
FOUR 162
FIVE 190

ACKNOWLEDGMENTS 223
CAPTIONS 224

WELCOME TO *BEHIND THE BLUE DOOR*—the ultimate expression of my lifelong passion for art and design. I invite you to join me on a tour of my home, which represents and reflects my personal aesthetic—a maximalist mantra.

I have worked in the fashion and beauty industries for decades, collaborating with some of the greatest entrepreneurs, creators, image makers, artists, and designers. Like many people, I have often been misunderstood. In my professional life, I have always been a suit to the creatives and a creative to the suits. But I have been fortunate to have had so many people contribute to my success and support my point of view. You see, I am actually a very private person, an introvert with an irrepressible desire to see the beauty in everything, from the most mundane to the extraordinary.

My personal journey began in the Midwest. I am the son of stylish, remarkable parents. My dad, Joe, was an industrialist with a love of architecture and design, and my mother, Renée, is an artist and fashion force. Together they pushed me to step out of my comfort zone, be unique, and stand for something. I have had many jobs and have lived in many homes. The evolution of my personal taste may not appeal to everyone, but my credo is a quest for continuous change and self-improvement, for fearless self-expression, for living life to the fullest. As a student of history, pop culture, and style, I have long been a champion of emerging talent—the unknown, unseen, and unheard.

I hope this book will provide a peek behind the doors of my dreams and passions and at the same time be an inspiration for others to find and define their own path. Embracing the possible and exploring the extraordinary has been my North Star. My dear friend Bibi Monnahan, who has been my interior designer for thirty years, and I have traveled the globe and the internet in search of the bold, the unusual, and the unexpected. Recently, I have learned that doors sometimes close, but there is always another that opens. Behind every door, every room, every object, there is another story, another world to be discovered. Each room, each object, each photograph converses with all the others—and with the ages. A home, like a life, is an organic entity, constantly evolving and informed by the past and the future. It does not matter where you start in life; everyone can create their own canvas. Perception is reality. The best advice I have ever received is "You do you." For me, that means imagination without guardrails. What does it mean for you?

Wishing you love, health, and happiness,

John

PREFACE

INTRODU

IF THERE'S

HELL IS EMPTY AND ALL THE DEVILS ARE HERE

MAN IN THE WORLD WHO EMBODIES THE MAXIMALIST MANTRA, IT'S JOHN DEMSEY.

As someone who has known (and adored) him for nearly a quarter century, I can tell you unequivocally the phrase "MORE IS MORE" WAS *INVENTED* FOR PEOPLE LIKE JOHN.

From the silk floral linings of his bespoke blazers to his blue suede shoes to his red-framed glasses, John is a man to whom rules do not apply.

"Imagination without guardrails," he says.

That philosophy extends to his madcap home.

After all, when have you ever seen a book devoted entirely to a single house?

Throughout these sumptuous pages, *Behind the Blue Door* examines a life well lived in a one-of-a-kind townhouse on Manhattan's Upper East Side.

A WORLD OF SUPERLATIVES, A FEAST FOR THE EYES.

To fully comprehend how John Demsey arrived at this unique aesthetic, you must first understand the environment in which he grew up and worked.

And let's not forget his love of fashion, an obsession that began early on when he insisted to his parents at age thirteen that he had to have a Pierre Cardin Nehru jacket, just like the Beatles, for his piano recital.

As a visionary beauty executive who spent more than thirty years at the Estée Lauder Companies, John grew MAC Cosmetics from a niche Canadian brand into a global behemoth, in large part by championing huge talents like Lady Gaga and Nicki Minaj long before they were household names.

It was John who convinced Tom Ford to make fragrances.

As it turns out, that was a very good idea.

Beauty is in his blood.

John was raised in Shaker Heights, Ohio, the son of an industrialist father with a love of mid-century modern design and a mod mother who wore hot pants and go-go boots and was the in-house artist at Bergdorf Goodman in the '70s and '80s.

Diana Vreeland famously said, "THE EYE MUST TRAVEL."

The Demsey family, John included, took that to heart.

It was as a college student studying in Paris that he first discovered his love of photography.

Perusing the Marché aux Puces, Paris's legendary flea market, he stumbled upon an early publicity photo of famed French siren Brigitte Bardot as a *brunette*.

It was then that he realized he could own a piece of glamour for just a few French francs.

Today, John is one of the most prominent collectors of photography in the world.

AND THE PHOTO OF BARDOT? It still hangs in his home today, just as meaningful as the Marilyn Minter, David LaChapelle, and Inez & Vinoodh photos that hang beside it.

THERE ARE 900 INDIVIDUAL PIECES OF ART HANGING ON THE WALLS. And that's just the beginning.

Over five floors of living space, John has packed every nook and cranny with objects of desire, custom David Hicks–inspired carpets, vintage furniture, and precious family heirlooms—an endless maze of discovery.

A surprise not just *Behind the Blue Door*, but behind every door . . . on every floor.

But what makes this house so special is the way in which the objects, colors, patterns, and textures—in all shapes and sizes—live together.

A place where John imagines Queen Elizabeth holding court with Grace Jones, with Lizzo, David Bowie, and Yayoi Kusama at the next table.

There are rooms within rooms, carefully assembled colorful vignettes—not unlike mini movie sets.

And not just color, but color that hits you smack in the face.

It's a *lot*, to be sure. But the overall effect is one of coherence, not clutter.

And the work is never done. The artwork alone is rehung twice a year. And furniture that may start on one floor, over time, is often moved to another. And, to think, IT ALL BEGAN WITH A PAIR OF SHOES.

Over dinner in Paris with Suzanne von Aichinger, the former model and muse to Galliano, John was in awe of his close friend's multicolored Louboutin boots. They reminded him, he says, of the glamorous Guy Bourdin era of the '70s.

Suddenly, the man who says he's as inspired by haute couture as he is by candy wrappers had an idea. He asked if he could take the boots home, which he did, and then promptly took them to Stark, which made all of the custom rugs in the house.

On display in the living room on the second floor is the carpet inspired by the boots.

From there, John took a dusty old Willy Rizzo couch covered in brown pigskin that once belonged to his parents and reupholstered the massive piece, which seats twenty-three, in lush blue velvet.

Repurposing plays a big role. The leopard-patterned chaise longue opposite the couch has been reupholstered three times.

But there's plenty of new. Like the Hugh Findletar Murano-glass vases of cartoon-like faces dotted throughout the house or the Ruan Hoffmann misshapen plates—there are more than a hundred of them—adorned with phrases like "Give it a rest" and "Don't worry, no one cares."

Or the bust of Brigitte Bardot as Marianne that he found, yes, back at the Marché aux Puces.

John is a man who thrives on discovery and finds just as much joy in the hunt as he does in the acquisition.

SHOP 'TIL YOU DROP IS HIS RALLYING CRY.

Once you've made your way through the book, you may ask yourself, "Who on earth would actually live here?"

To that, John says, "WITHIN THE PATTERN OF THE CHAOS, I FIND MY CALM."

Have fun, don't take yourself so seriously.

There's a valuable life lesson here. MAYBE, JUST MAYBE, YOU'LL BE INSPIRED.

She imagined herself a starlet.

FLOOR

ONE

"YOU NEVER GET A SECOND CHANCE TO MAKE A FIRST IMPRESSION."

If you thought for a moment that you'd be easing into the drama that is the Demsey townhouse, think again. *Behind the Blue Door*, on Floor One, is your first glimpse of the high-octane glamour that infuses every inch of this packed-to-the-gills house.

It's where you begin to understand just how obsessed John is with the idea of collecting—plates, vases, animal figurines, even cookie jars. If there's a series of special items on offer, John's buying them. All of them. In every color, shape, and size.

Beyond the foyer, you'll find the kitchen, dining room, and sunroom. It's where weekends are spent eating and lounging; it's also where some of John's best parties start and end.

After all, what screams *party* more than a lit-from-within mirrored chest by Patrick Naggar that has pride of place in the dining room? And what says *fashion* more than the blue leather Hermès chair or the Inez & Vinoodh one-of-a-kind photo collage that hangs above it?

There are plenty of nods to John's career in beauty too. A life-sized glamour shot of Gisele Bündchen by Mario Testino greets you at the door. Next to it is a sexy image of parted lips by Marilyn Minter and a *Rolling Stone* cover photo of Dua Lipa by David LaChapelle. And let's not forget the acid-hued mise-en-scène photographs by Miles Aldridge. They're *everywhere*.

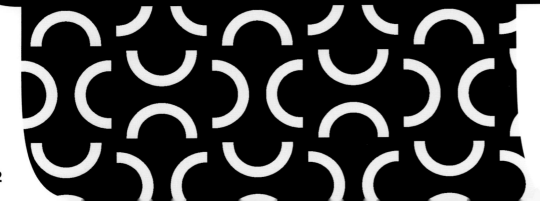

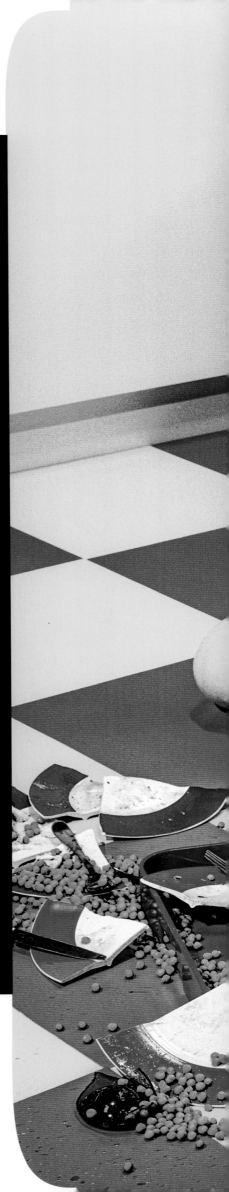

"JOHN'S HOME IS AN EXERCISE IN ORGANIZED ECLECTICISM THAT SHOWS HIS EXUBERANT SENSE OF HUMOR AND VIVID SENSE OF COLOR. THE HOUSE FOR US REFLECTS HIS UNCOMPROMISING WAY OF LOOKING AT LIFE AND AT THE ARTISTS HE BELIEVES IN WITH A STRONG PUSH TOWARD CONTINUOUS INNOVATION AND A CONTAGIOUS CURIOSITY FOR ALL THAT MAKES THE YOUNGER GENERATION TICK."

—INEZ & VINOODH

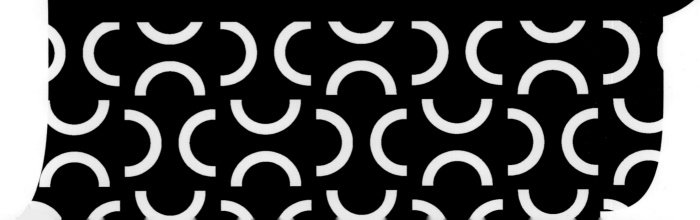

Highly saturated color plays a big role. So does humor. Just look at his vast collection of Ruan Hoffmann plates. Or the countless crazy creature sculptures atop every available surface. Or the cookie jars made in the likenesses of Cher, Chaka Khan, and Ruth Bader Ginsburg.

His love of mid-century modern design is on full display alongside family heirlooms. In the sunroom, you'll find a pair of Eames chairs, reupholstered in yellow leather, that once sat in John's father's office. On the chairs, needlepoint pillows made by his grandmother.

Then there's the kitchen. For many, it's an afterthought—a place where you take a break from design in favor of function. Not here. Hanging on the narrow strip of wall high above the range is his collection of rare Fornasetti calendar plates. On a nearby wall, Sardi's-like portraits of his pet family by artist Kathy Hoets. Who does that, you ask? John Demsey.

If you stop and think for a moment about the sheer number of items on display, it might make your head spin. But the mash-up, the result of a painstaking decision-making process that can take days, if not weeks, is what makes this house so unique.

"There's always another layer," says John. A maximalist mantra, to be sure.

She imagined herself a starlet.

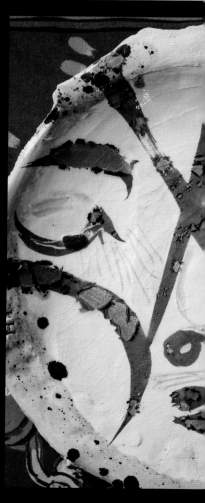

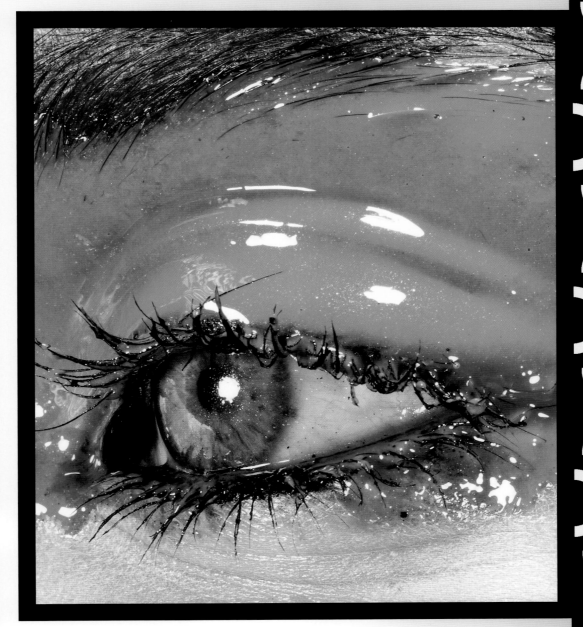
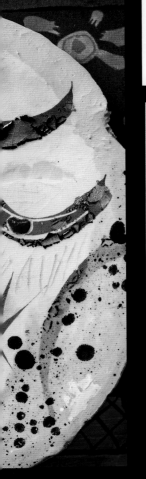

"VIBRANT! COLORFUL! ECLECTIC! UNUSUAL! FANTASTICAL! UNIQUE! JUST A FEW ADJECTIVES THAT COME TO MIND WHEN GAZING AT THE PAGES OF PHOTOGRAPHS OF JOHN DEMSEY'S ONE-OF-A-KIND NEW YORK CITY HOME. IT'S HARD TO IMAGINE, BUT I DO NOT THINK I HAVE EVEN ONE ITTY-BITTY LIKE OBJECT IN ANY OF MY HOMES!"

—MARTHA STEWART

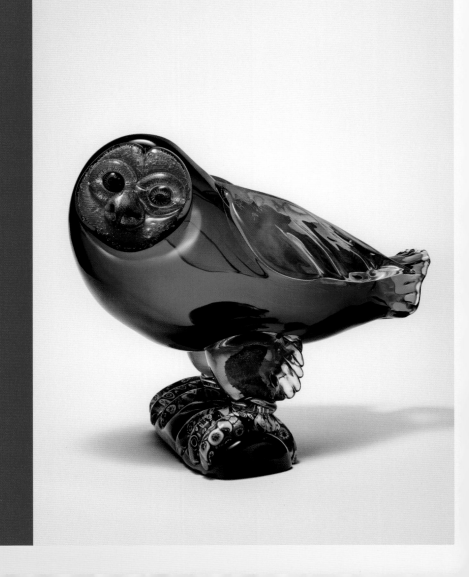

CHINESE ART

MATTIA BONETTI

FASHIONING MASCULINITIES

NEW YORK INTERIORS SIMON UPTON

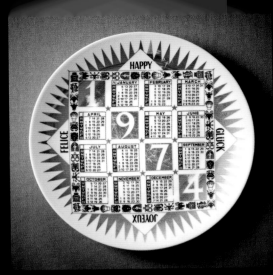

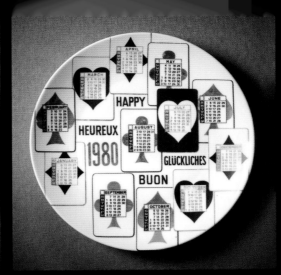

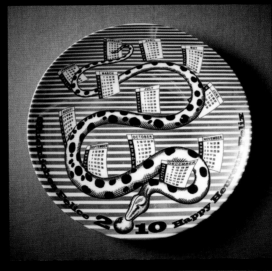

FLOOR

TWO

IN A HOME FULL OF SHOWSTOPPING ROOMS, THE LIVING ROOM ON FLOOR TWO IS QUITE POSSIBLY THE SHOW-STOPPER OF THEM ALL.

What you'll find here is the juxtaposition of glamour, celebrity, and high society, spanning from the 1940s to the present. It's pop culture personified, a place where the most famous faces in the world are on the walls, exchanging glances, crisscrossing generations, having imaginary conversations about who and what came before and who is emerging now.

It's a room where Frank Sinatra and Mia Farrow chat with Kim Kardashian and David Bowie. Where Lizzo and Cardi B sip tea with Gloria Vanderbilt and Queen Elizabeth. The common thread? Grace Jones, the ringleader. To be a fly on the wall.

It's a showcase of John's most prized photographs, a place where he exhibits the work of personal friends like Ellen von Unwerth, Jean-Paul Goude, and the late Roxanne Lowit. And the stars on the wall? Many of them are friends of John too.

This blue-on-blue-on-blue wonder of a room tricks the eye in endless ways.

LIVING ROOM

Take color, for example. I dare you to count the number of blue hues. At first glance, you might think all the different shades of blue clash. But upon closer inspection, you begin to notice that the seemingly clashing shades actually complement one another.

There's a method to the madness, after all.

If you look skyward, you'll see the midnight-blue Baccarat chandelier by Philippe Starck. But almost indiscernible to the naked eye is the fact that the shades are made of denim. That's right. Think blue jeans. On a lampshade. In a formal living room.

The centerpiece of this expansive room is a huge blue crushed-velvet Willy Rizzo couch that once belonged to John's parents. And let's not forget the wall-to-wall Stark custom carpet inspired by those multicolored Christian Louboutin boots. Remember, it all started with those boots.

There are examples everywhere of John's collecting prowess, like the Niki de Saint Phalle *Nana* sculpture—displayed in the atrium—that he bought long before her work was considered collectible. Or the Vincenzo De Cotiis coffee table he found in Milan long before anyone had heard of him. Atop the table, a veritable animal kingdom, including a giant hippopotamus bought at the Marché aux Puces in Paris and a panther head acquired from the estate of late studio executive Brad Grey.

There are vases by Baccarat and Venini—barware too. And Asprey crystal decanters with animal stoppers. It's all in the details.

Above the door leading into the library, a long row of David Bailey prints of, among others, Mick Jagger, John Lennon, and Paul McCartney. Above them, more Ruan Hoffmann misshapen plates.

Like the rest of the house, not one square inch is left empty. Why would it be? That would be boring. And boring this house is not.

"I FEEL LIKE I NEED A MEMBERSHIP CARD TO GET IN," said one of John's chicest friends upon entering the library. The ultimate compliment.

John's original idea for the library was to create a cozy space that looks and feels like a private club in London. It's an homage to legendary nightclub owner Mark Birley, of Annabel's fame, a man John calls the ultimate purveyor of over-the-top British taste.

The red room, as it's called, is a space John describes as "surrealism to the max." Of course, the idea of surrealism exists throughout the house, but it's especially evident here—a seemingly irrational mash-up of objects, patterns, and colors. Yet somehow, as in the best surrealist art, it all comes together in a dreamlike way.

And, if you haven't figured it out already, when it comes to a theme, John is all in. He doesn't do anything halfway.

Underneath the giant Charles Paris Bubbles chandelier is the David Hicks–patterned red, pink, and orange carpet from Stark. Sitting on top, the Christian Liaigre sofa reupholstered in Hermès orange—a couch for lounging; it's a "club," after all. And let's not forget the tripartite Guy de Rougemont Golden Clover coffee table, hard to get and unique, like so many other objects in the house.

Almost every piece of art in the library is framed in gold. Speaking of which, you could say the pièce de résistance is the "Black Is Beautiful" poster by Kwame Brathwaite, the American photojournalist and activist who popularized the phrase. There are three works by Brathwaite hanging in the room, one on top of the other.

LIBRARY

On a high shelf next to the window, you'll find a Daum decorative object by Salvador Dalí. On a nearby wall, a shocking Steven Klein photograph of a blue Nicki Minaj with bubble gum–pink hair. And don't miss the Laurie Hogin painting of a furry monkey grasping a tube of lipstick. A surrealist mix, to be sure.

Then, there's what John calls the "cabinet of curiosities"—objects as varied as a leaded-glass form of Lenin that he bought in Poland next to an Oscar-like statue of photographer Terry Richardson. His love of animals is everywhere too, from the Baccarat jungle cats on a shelf to the large Hugh Findletar green owl on the mantel. Next to the owl, a vintage gold lion clutch by Judith Leiber that once belonged to his mother.

Once again, his love of fashion is on display, from the Gucci needle-point pillows to the Hermès throws to the Fornasetti plates for Louis Vuitton hanging on the fireplace to the decorative bird plucked straight from the Christmas windows at Bergdorf Goodman.

Just off the library is a jewel box of a powder room filled with illustrations by Donald Robertson, a child-sized Mia Fonssagrives-Solow robot, and an Orrefors chandelier from his childhood home; it was part of his mother's wedding trousseau.

As always, the overall look is one of cohesion, a merging of John's passion for objects and art that make you think with reminders everywhere that nothing is more important than family.

"JOHN DEMSEY'S HOME ENGAGES THE SENSES AS SOON AS YOU WALK THROUGH THE DOOR; THE ARTWORK, THE COLORS, THE LAYERS OF TEXTURES CREATE AN ECLECTIC WONDERLAND THAT TRANSPORTS YOU. "

—NAOMI CAMPBELL

Harland Miller

all glam

FL(O)(O)R

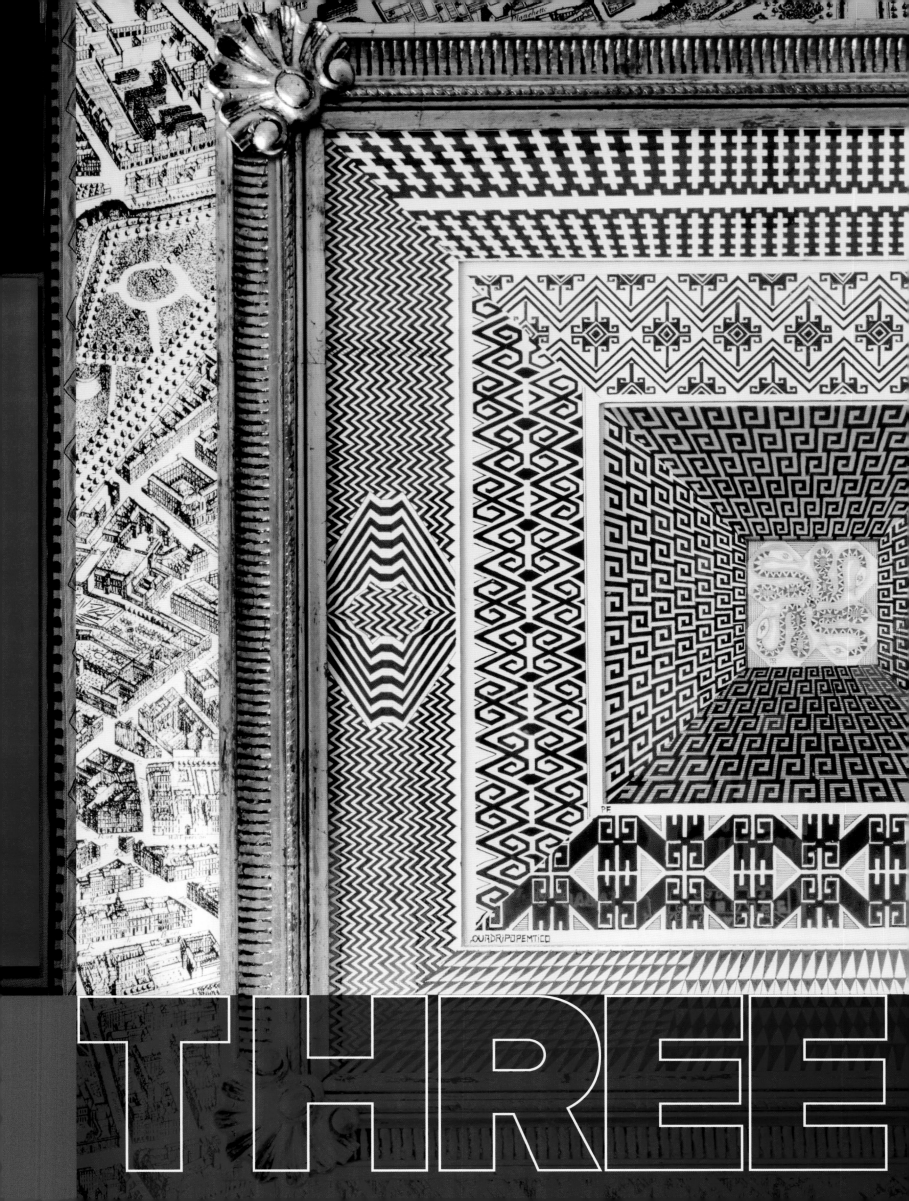

THREE

FOR AS LONG AS I'VE KNOWN JOHN DEMSEY, HE'S ALWAYS SAID, "WEEK-DAYS ARE FOR WORK, WEEKENDS FOR FRIENDS." It's a reference to how he manages his evening plans. Using the same logic, you could say that Floor Three is the "weekend" floor. The most personal floor in the house, it's an intimate space only his closest friends have seen.

After leaving the nightlife and club vibe of the floors below, where John has hosted countless parties for hundreds at a time, Floor Three is where you'll find his office, his bedroom, and his prized dressing room. Even the hallway is personal, its walls filled with artwork, like the red-and-white print splashed with the phrase "I shop therefore I am," and family photos, including a Yousuf Karsh portrait of John at age twenty-one. John's father commissioned the work from the late Karsh, one of the greatest portrait photographers of the twentieth century.

The office is an homage to Paris, where John lived as a college student, his first stay in a foreign country, far away from his native Midwest. So there was much to be discovered in the City of Light. Paris is where John first became enraptured by all of life's possibilities. It's also where he began to form his now signature sartorial style. And so, the references to all things French are everywhere, down to the walls. The Schumacher wallpaper is an actual map of Paris. Next to the desk is a vintage model of the Eiffel Tower from Ralph Lauren Home. Around the room, a Jean Cocteau plate, an Yves Klein–blue bust, and photos of Picasso in Cannes and Kate Moss at the famed Brasserie Lipp. The now familiar Ruan Hoffmann plates in the office are adorned with French obscenities. As I've said, John leans into a theme. Big time.

On the opposite side of the floor is his bedroom, where the dominant shade is red, his favorite color, and the dominant pattern is leopard, which John calls a "neutral." It is, really. Here, you see his sense of humor at play. Monkey business is everywhere. On the wall between the windows is a Mark Gagnon painting of John as a monkey, his favorite animal, wearing—what else?—a Thom Browne suit. To the side of the bed, a giant Richard Orlinski red gorilla sculpture, one of eight Orlinski gorillas in the house. There are nods to his beauty career too, of course. And all of the hardware here is by his good friend Lisa Eisner. After all, details matter, down to the doorknobs.

Then there's the eye-popping dressing room, a feature John says he's wanted his entire life. I mean, honestly, have you ever seen anything like it? The hundreds of custom shirts are organized by color, many by Parisian shirtmaker Charvet, the oldest shirt shop in the world. On the walls, custom sketches by master tailors at Zegna, Berluti, and Taillour. On the dresser, sunglasses by Morgenthal Frederics and Jacques Marie Mage and fragrances by Tom Ford and Frédéric Malle, fragrance brands John championed. There are shoes by John Lobb and Berluti; even the sock drawer is special. It's a bespoke world like no other. A fashion lover's dream.

FOLIES PIGALLE
PARIS BY NIGHT

FOLIES PIGALLE
PARIS BY NIGHT

KUMA

A PASSION FOR INTERIORS Carolyne Roehm

VLADIMIR KAGAN A LIFETIME OF AVANT-GARDE DESIGN

YAMAMOTO & YOHJI

BORN TO PARTY FORCED TO WORK

Editions de Parfums Frédéric Malle The First Twenty Years

Signature SPACES WELL-TRAVELLED INTERIORS BY PAOLO MOSCHINO & PHILIP VERGEYLEN

Ermenegildo Zegna Skira

ONALD ASSOULINE

T FLYING ASSOULINE

JANN S. WENNER LIKE A ROLLING STONE A memoir

Philippe Garner sixties design TASCHEN

ED RUSCHA PHOTOGRAPHER

WHERE'S KARL

PHILIP JOHNSON

THE MEN'S FAS

... john is a true individual ... the way he lives is truly his own ... the way he dresses is truly his own ... what he surrounds himself with is truly his own ... he is someone who inspires ... he has championed true creatives before anyone else knew of them ... even the creatives themselves ... anyone who has ever had the good fortune to spend time with John is truly fortunate ... this time with John and his true and unique individuality is life changing ...

—THOM BROWNE

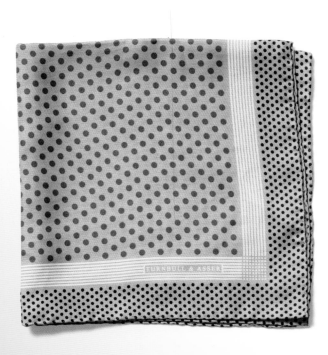

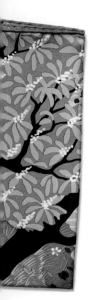

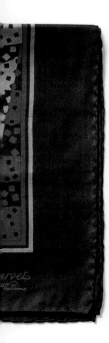

FLOOOR

FOUR

DO YOU SENSE A SHIFT IN THE VIBE?

By now, you already know that each floor in the Demsey townhouse has an overarching theme—each room too. Like Floor Three, Floor Four is personal, but this one is all about girl power with a decidedly more feminine palette.

Here, four generations of women in John's family are represented, from his great-grandmother to his grandmother to his artist mother to his beloved teenage daughter. It's where you'll find his daughter's bedroom and two guest bedrooms, which serve as de facto gallery spaces for John's mother's distinctive floral paintings.

For two decades, in the 1970s and '80s, Renée Demsey was the in-house artist at Bergdorf Goodman. Her artwork was sold at the store, in an area called Nena's Choice Gallery. An arts patron and philanthropist, Nena Manach Goodman was the wife of Andrew Goodman, owner and chairman of Bergdorf Goodman in the 1950s and '60s. Renée was incredibly prolific, creating roughly five thousand paintings over many decades. And just recently, at age ninety, she took up drawing again. And so, the whole floor is a love letter to Renée, a riot of flowers, colors, and patterns inspired by her work.

Your first hint of what's to come is at the top of the staircase—the ultimate in feminine imagery. On the wall, two photographs of plumped-up lips—one in shiny red, the other in glossy pink—by Terry Richardson. To the left are the guest bedrooms, kaleidoscopes of color from top to bottom.

All around the "Renée guest suites," as John calls them, there are conversation pieces, like the yellow Vincent Darré Conversation chair (its blue cousin is on Floor One), Gio Ponti desk, and Gucci Décor chair. On the walls, of course, are Renée's paintings. In the windows, there are vintage Murano-glass vases in one room, a vintage Scandinavian monkey figurine in the other. Framing it all, Kelly Wearstler wallpaper and—you know the drill—David Hicks–patterned Stark carpets.

On the other end of the floor is daughter Marie Helene's bedroom, arguably the most feminine room in the entire house—a room all about family ties. On the bed, needlepoint pillows made by John's mother and grandmother. Above the desk, an ornate mirror that once belonged to John's great-grandmother. There are plenty of fashionable touches too—most notably, a huge Lanvin mirror hand painted by the fashion house's late designer Alber Elbaz.

Even the powder rooms are worth a mention. From the floral wallpaper to the D. Porthault towels to the Terry O'Neill black-and-white photos of Audrey Hepburn, the bathrooms get as much special attention as every other room in the house. Why wouldn't they? We're talking about John Demsey. Everywhere you look, there is beauty.

"JOHN DEMSEY IS A TRUE GENTLEMAN, FULL OF STYLE, CHARM, AND GRACE. HE IS ALSO FIERCELY INTELLIGENT, A SHARP WIT, BEAUTIFULLY DRESSED, AND WELL MANNERED. IN HIS HOME HE HAS CREATED A MAGICAL PLACE— MODERN, TRADITIONAL, TRUE CANDY FOR ALL THE SENSES. TO SAY HE HAS GREAT TASTE IS PUTTING IT MILDLY."

—CORNELIA GUEST

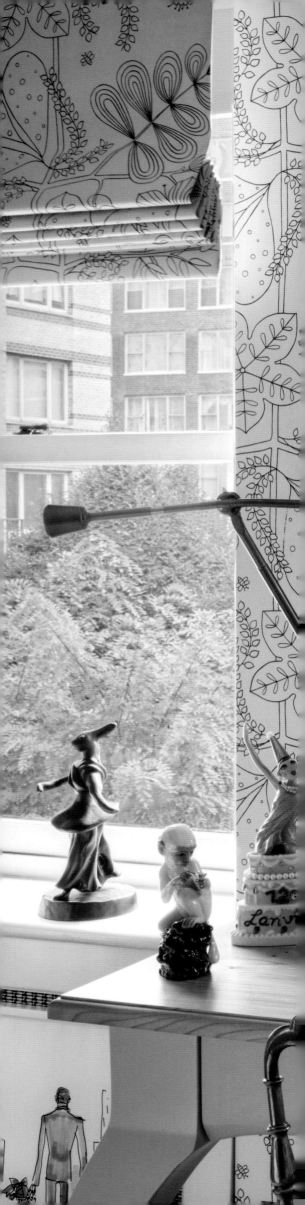

FLOOR

FIVE

"IT'S ACTUALLY THE MOST MINIMALIST FLOOR." That's how John responded, with a straight face, when I asked him to describe Floor Five. He's not kidding. In his maximalist world of design, the floor at the top of the house *is* more minimal than the rest. After all, you can see the tops of the tables. Sort of. And everything is relative, right?

Floor Five is an homage to Andy Warhol's Factory, the artist's studio that served as a chic hangout for other artists, musicians, and celebrities in the 1960s and '70s—the famous and the infamous. So, Warhol and '60s references are everywhere, from the Andrew Unangst photograph of the artist holding a Campbell's soup can to the Roy Lichtenstein–inspired artwork to the Pucci pillows. It's all part of the mix.

On this floor—which is almost like a loft apartment—you'll find the sitting room, where father and daughter hang out on weekends. Then there's the tricked-out gym, where John spends an hour a day, seven days a week, pumping iron. Floor Five is also where John's two cats live, cat and dog relations being what they are. The eight dogs, in case you're wondering, stay mostly on Floor One. Family harmony is key.

The staircase leading up to Floor Five is lined with calming imagery, reflecting John's love of travel and escape and offering a brief respite from the riotous color above and below. The mirrored horse head that greets you at the top is another acquisition from Bergdorf Goodman's Christmas windows, circa 2017. Rule of thumb: even if it's not for sale, ask anyway. There's a good chance you might be able to buy it.

In the sitting room, many of John's favorite designers are on repeat: Fornasetti vases, Gucci pillows, Ruan Hoffmann plates, and Miles Aldridge photographs at every turn. Sprinkled in, a Willy Rizzo chrome lamp here, a Curtis Jeré *Sputnik* sculpture there.

The gym is its own crazy, art-filled world. Once you get past the custom workout equipment trimmed in red leather, you'll find mirrored walls blanketed with graffiti art and photographs of '60s icons like Twiggy and Warren Beatty. The centerpiece of the room is an original Steven Klein photograph of Daphne Guinness, a former spokesmodel for MAC Cosmetics. John is credited with putting MAC on the map.

Floor Five took some time to take shape. It began as a place where items that didn't fit or work in other parts of the house would end up. The pink India Mahdavi chair, once in Marie Helene's bedroom, is now here. And so is the Jayde Cardinalli black-and-white print of John's pets, which was originally on Floor One. Like so many things, over time the floor found itself and blossomed into something beautiful, much like the Missoni floral-print carpet reproduced by Stark.

The same could be said for the entire home. Constantly evolving, the Demsey townhouse is always morphing into a better version of itself. A place where life is never boring and there's always more than meets the eye.

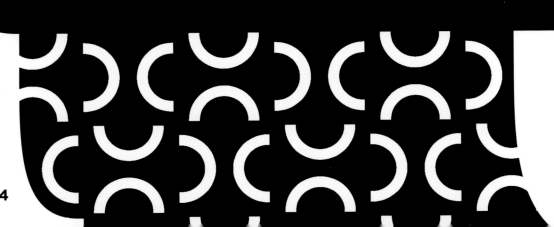

THE FASHION BOOK

NINA CAMPBELL INTERIOR DECORATION

Shifting Paradigms in Contemporary Ceramics

FRANÇOIS HALARD

LORI GOLDSTEIN STYLE IS INSTINCT

MONEY PEOPLE POWER MARCO GROB

B A L S

MARTIN SCHOELLER PORTRAITS

BUNNIES Hunt Slonem

DEDICATION

BEHIND THE BLUE DOOR is dedicated to my mother, Renée, and my late father, Joseph. To the joy of my life, my daughter, Marie Helene Demsey, and her mother, Anouschka. To my sister, Mary Jo Friedman, her husband, Freddy, and my niece and nephew, Molly and Tom Friedman. To my unconditional emotional support squad: Scout, Olivia, Dora, Gizmo, Bella, Sugar, Diego, Zeus, Biscuit, and Roxy.

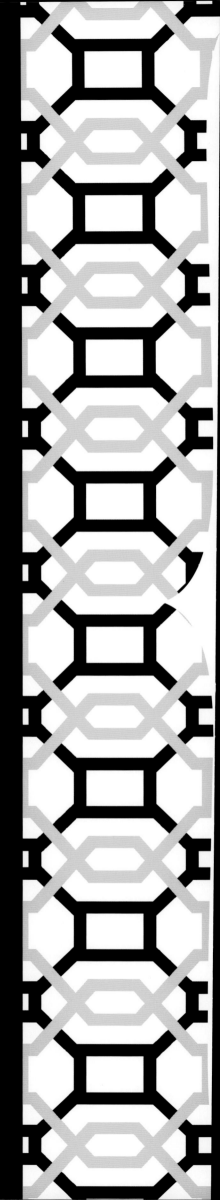

ACKNOWLEDGMENTS

I AM DEEPLY GRATEFUL TO THE FOLLOWING, WITHOUT WHOM THIS BOOK WOULD NOT HAVE BEEN POSSIBLE:

1. *Behind the Blue Door* creative team: photographer Douglas Friedman and his assistant Kit Sinclair; author Alina Cho; stylist Mieke ten Have; objects photographer Ethan Herrington.

2. Vendome Press: publishers Beatrice Vincenzini and Mark Magowan; editor Jacqueline Decter; designer Rita Sowins; production director Jim Spivey.

3. HOME DESIGN: Bibi Monnahan, interior design; Heather McKenna Pardo, art design; Joseph Cornacchia, AIA, architecture; Marko Matijas, floral design; Alex Mednikov, Stark Carpet; David Michael, window treatments; Paul Deutsch, Houston Upholstery; Dayne Christian, construction; Apparatus Studio, lighting.

4. MY NORTH STAR: Leonard Lauder.

5. ARTISTS/CREATORS: Miles Aldridge, Sylvie Blum, Huge Findletar, Ruan Hoffmann, David LaChapelle, and every other photographer, artist, sculptor, artisan, and designer whose work appears on these pages—too numerous to list individually.

6. ALL OF THOSE WHO ALWAYS SHOW UP: Kelly Bensimon, Tony Brand and Linda Fargo, Mary Ann Browning, Naomi Campbell, Alina Cho, Jennifer Creel, Beverly Durham, Arabella Ferrari, Dario Ferrari, Bobby Fomon and Jill Fairchild, Martha and Neal Fox, James Gager, Maria Garcia, Marilyn Gauthier, Muriel Gonzalez, Stephanie George, Mike Gould, Cornelia Guest, Sara and Patrick Handreke, Marcus Henderson, JHH, Jessica Joffe, T. Bryan Karasu, M.D., Jill Kargman, Dr. Andreas Kraebber, Melanie Kusin, Marina Maher, Jackie Mella, Bibi Monnahan, Susana Morales, Lora and Kevin Nee, Danny Nunz, Jakob and Vanessa Panotas, Junior Poncheo, Edie and Robert Parker, Jolene Postley, Judy and Peter Price, Donald Robertson, Michael and B.Z. Schwartz, Susan Silver, Laura and Harry Slatkin, Howard Socol, Leslie Stoval, Stephen and Emily Strick, Blaine Trump and Steve Simon, Inez van Lamsweerde and Vinoodh Matadin, Priscilla Waters, Danielle Westcott, Paul Wilmot.

PAGES 2–3: Second-floor atrium.

PAGES 4–5: Detail, fifth-floor "Factory" sitting room.

PAGES 6–7: Detail, second-floor living room.

PAGE 8: The blue door, designed by architect Joseph Cornacchia and featuring a vintage lion's-head knocker, painted with sixteen coats of Benjamin Moore's high-gloss Caribbean Blue.

PAGE 12: John Demsey, dressed in a custom Berluti suit, in his living room.

PAGES 14–15: Vintage publicity photo of Brigitte Bardot, sourced at Marché aux Puces, Paris; multicolored Louboutin boots, the inspiration for the palette of the custom living room carpet by Stark.

PAGE 16: The Connor Brothers, *Hell Is Empty and All the Devils Are Here*, 2017.

FLOOR ONE

PAGES 22–23: Miles Aldridge, *I Only Want You to Love Me #1*, 2011.

PAGES 24–25: Dining room. Hervé Van der Straeten, Lustre Volubile 306 chandelier; Patrick Naggar, mirrored, internally lit Spinoza chest.

PAGE 26: Top: Miles Aldridge, *Hello*, 2020; bottom: Miles Aldridge, *I Will Love You Tomorrow*, 2020.

PAGES 28–29: Top left: Marcia Resnick, *She Imagined Herself a Starlet*, 1976–77; center: Rankin, *Enigma*, 2011; top right: William Klein, *Antonia in a Mirror Box, Paris*, 1963; bottom right: Bert Stern, *David Bailey and Veruschka, VOGUE, New York*, 1964; Baccarat, crystal vase with band of gilded tigers; Nymphenburg, rhinoceros "Clara" in white bisque; Christofle, silver hawk and silver horse; Mario Botta, GEO crystal vase for Lalique.

PAGE 30: Ruan Hoffmann, plate.

PAGE 31: Top left: William Klein, fashion photo; bottom left: William Klein, *Nina + Simone, Piazza di Spagna, Rome*, 1960; right: Inez & Vinoodh, *Fashion Plate no. 12 (Fragments)*, 2021; Hermès, blue leather chair; Karl Springer, torch lamp.

PAGES 32–33: Overview of dining room. India Mahdavi dining tables; Fornasetti, black leather chairs; Franz West, metal-framed chairs with bands of African fabrics. On the tables: L'Objet Haas Brothers, *Haas Pedro the Croc Box*; Jean René Gauguin, painted ceramic tiger; Hugh Findletar, Murano-glass Flowerheadz vases and horse head.

PAGE 34: Studio Job, *Black Cat*, 2013, polished and patinated bronze, LED lighting.

PAGE 35: Center: Roe Ethridge, *Emily Baker*, 2017; top right: Guy Bourdin photo for French *Vogue*, 1978; bottom left: Elliott Erwitt, *New York City*, 1974; bottom right: Thandiwe Muriu, *CAMO 20*, 2021; Vladimir Kagan, blue leather chair; Christofle, silver obelisk; Libertine, needle-point pillow.

PAGES 36–37: India Mahdavi, pedestal; Daniele Fortuna, *Radio Gaga*; Hugh Findletar, Flowerheadz vase; Ruan Hoffmann, plate; Ben Hassett, photo of eye for *Harper's Bazaar* (unpublished), 2015, and portrait with yellow background for *Vogue Japan*, 2015.

PAGES 38–39: In front of fireplace: Stefan Rinck, *Ballplayer #1*, 2013; Massimiliano Pelletti, stratified-stone bust; Jeff Koons, *Puppy (Vase)*, 1998.

PAGES 40–41: Hervé Van der Straeten, Mirror Solaire 365; Hugh Findletar, Murano-glass horse head and Flowerheadz vase; Daum, covered vessel; Baccarat, black panther; Baccarat, pair of Harcourt Our Fire crystal candlesticks with metallic-finish shades; Lalique, Bacchantes vase.

PAGE 42: Ruan Hoffmann, plate.

PAGE 43: Vincent Darré, Conversation chair; Maison Christian Dior, silver monkey; Warren Platner, side table.

PAGES 44–45: Selection of the 125 Ruan Hoffmann plates in John Demsey's collection, the largest in private hands.

PAGES 46–47: Center right: Josef Jasso, *Black Marilyn*; bottom right: Jane Black, watercolor of sunroom; Ruan Hoffmann, gold figurines.

PAGE 48–48A: Sunroom. Pierre Frey, Vue d'en haut wallpaper; Sara Cwynar, *Tracy Stepping Forward*, 2017 (left) and *Flower*, 2017 (right); Guy de Rougemont, totem; Fornasetti, striped credenza; Boris Tabakoff, Armlesschair; Atang Tshikare, Maotwana Finyela (bronze bench with lights).

PAGE 48B, CLOCKWISE FROM TOP LEFT: Lladró, Blue Gold Gorilla; Russell Wrankle, Red Hare, 2012; Hugh Findletar, Patook owl; Jean-Louis Sauvat, Balthazar horse for Daum.

ANIMALS GATEFOLD OPENER: Left: William Klein, *Hat & 5 Roses, Paris (Vogue)*, 1956.

ANIMALS GATEFOLD: 1st row: Daum, silver reindeer; Baccarat, black panther; Tony Duquette, Ghost Snail light; Maurizio Galante, parrot; 2nd row: Daum, blue crocodile; Isabelle Carabantes, Savana elephant for Daum; Madeleine van der Knoop, peacock for Daum; Venini, glass tiger; Richard Orlinski, Wild Bear in amber for Daum; 3rd row: Viktor Schreckengost, blue ceramic bull; Isabelle Carabantes, Cogito monkey; 4th row: hippopotamus, sourced at Marché aux Puces, Paris; African horned animal, sourced from Maison Gerard, Paris.

BACK OF ANIMALS GATEFOLD–PAGE 49: Fornasetti, vase; Katie Stout, blue figurine and purple lamp; Ruan Hoffmann, gold lion head and multicolored ceramic owl; Aldo Londi for Leclaireur, ceramic lion head; L'Objet Haas Brothers, *Haas Monster Ball Incense Burner*.

PAGES 50–51: Framed limited-edition Hermès scarf, designed by Hiroshi Sugimoto; pair of Eames chairs that belonged to John's father, reupholstered in yellow leather; leopard and tiger needlepoint pillows by Beatrice Mishel, John's maternal grandmother; Hunt Slonem, yellow bunny sculpture.

PAGE 52: Apparatus Studio, floor lamp; Donald Robertson, watercolor of John and dogs.

PAGE 53: Enrique Perezalba Red, Minnie and Mickey Mouse as foo dogs; bust of Brigitte Bardot as Marianne, symbol of France, sourced at Marché aux Puces, Paris; Ruan Hoffmann, gold sculpture.

PAGES 54–55: Kitchen. Fornasetti, plates; L'Objet Haas Brothers, black and white pitchers.

PAGES 56–57: Hazy Mae cookie jars, from left: Grace Jones, Jean-Michel Basquiat, Iris Apfel, Chaka Khan (black), Queen Elizabeth II, Ruth Bader Ginsburg, Chaka Khan (white), Cher, Audrey Hepburn; nesting dolls, sourced from Caviar Kaspia; Lladró, striped macaw; vintage Murano-glass parrots; Hugh Findletar, Flowerheadz vase; Richard Orlinski, white gorilla.

PAGE 58: Fornasetti, trays and calendar plates; vintage orange glassware from John's mother's trousseau, 1954; Christofle, silver egg; Dolce & Gabbana, candle housed in a hand-painted ceramic vase shaped like a Sicilian head; Michael Graves for Alessi, tea kettle.

PAGE 59: Kathy Hoets, dog and cat portraits, 1st row: Bella, Portia, Gizmo; 2nd row: Dora, Roxy, Mr. Pink; 3rd row: Olivia, Scout; 4th row: Diego, Mocha; 5th row: Biscuit, Sugar; bottom: Biscuit; Fornasetti, chair.

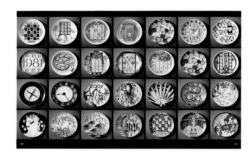

PAGES 60–61: Fornasetti, selection of vintage calendar plates.

PAGES 62–63: Dining area of kitchen. Apparatus Studio, ceiling fixture; Miles Aldridge, photos on left wall; Eero Saarinen, table; Warren Platner, chairs; La DoubleJ, table setting; Fornasetti, mounted plates; Davis Factor, photo of John and his daughter, Marie Helene; vintage bull's head that belonged to John's parents, painted bronze.

PAGE 64: Miles Aldridge, *New Utopias #1*, 2018.

PAGE 65: Top left: Miles Aldridge, *Extravagant Sophisticated Lady #5*, 2011; bottom left: Hermès, framed limited-edition silk fabric; top right: Tony Kelly, *Diretto per Roma*, 2020; bottom right: Tony Kelly, *Flight TK75*, 2014.

PAGE 66: First-floor hallway. Left: Mario Testino, *Gisele Bündchen*, 2007; top center: Marilyn Minter, *Bad Habit*, 2018; stair carpet in David Hicks pattern, reproduced by Stark.

PAGE 67: David LaChapelle, *Dua Lipa: Future Nostalgia*, 2020.

FLOOR TWO: LIVING ROOM

PAGES 70–71: Top left: Ellen von Unwerth, *Bienvenue, LA*, 2004; bottom left: Willy Rizzo, *Catherine Deneuve*; top right: Greg Gorman, *Mick Jagger and Bette Midler*, 1983; bottom right: Roxanne Lowit, *Speak No Evil, Hear No Evil, See No Evil* (Linda Evangelista, Naomi Campbell, Christy Turlington).

PAGES 72–73: Top left: Vikky Alexander, *Between Dreaming & Living V*, 1985; Top right: Chris Levine, *Lightness of Being*, 2010; bottom: Jean-Paul Goude, *An Androgynous Grace Jones*, 1981.

PAGES 74–75: 1st row, left: Patrick McMullan, *Grace Jones*; third from left: Roxanne Lowit, *Yves Saint Laurent and Diana Vreeland*; fourth from left: Ellen von Unwerth, *Hollywood*, 2011; 2nd row, center: Harry Benson, *Frank Sinatra and Mia Farrow at Truman Capote's "Black and White" Ball at the Plaza Hotel, New York*, 1966; 3rd row, center: Rose Hartman, *Bianca Jagger's 30th Birthday Party at Studio 54*, 1977; Willy Rizzo, couch; Vincenzo De Cotiis, coffee table; Campana Brothers for Louis Vuitton's Objets Nomades collection, Merengue pouf; Christopher Kreiling, Philodendron Leaf Lounge Chair; Hervé Van der Straeten, red Epines 23 lamp.

PAGE 76: Top left: Coreen Simpson, *Eartha Kitt, NYC*, 1978/2021; top center: Christopher Makos, *My Favorite Portrait of Andy Warhol*, 1986; top right: Kwame Brathwaite, *Untitled (Grace Jones)*; bottom left: Ellen von Unwerth, *Smashing, LA*, 2017; Pedro Friedeberg, Hand Foot chair.

PAGE 77: Miles Aldridge, *Night Car #3*, 2015.

PAGE 78: Richard Orlinski, blue gorilla; Tokujin Yoshioka, Blossom vase for Louis Vuitton.

PAGE 79: Hippopotamus, sourced at Marché aux Puces, Paris; vintage Murano-glass tortoise; Lalique, red snake.

PAGE 80: Estate of Brad Grey, panther head; Harvey Bouterse, eagle vase.

PAGE 81: Bottom left: Willy Rizzo, photo of Alfred Hitchcock at Cannes, 1965; top right: Greg Gorman, *Sophia Loren, Rome*, 1994; bottom right: Alix Malka, *Kim Kardashian*, art direction by Manfred Thierry Mugler; Jedd Novatt, yellow totem floor lamp; Schumacher, Cheetah-print pillows.

PAGES 82–83: Overview of living room and atrium. Philippe Starck for Baccarat, midnight-blue Zénith chandelier with denim shades; Benjamin Moore, custom blue wall color; David Hicks carpet pattern, reproduced by Stark in the colors of a pair of suede Louboutin boots.

PAGE 84: De Gournay, hand-painted screen; vintage foo dog.

PAGE 85: Vladimir Kagan, chair upholstered in Schumacher's Robert Burns pattern; Prada, blue-green dog figurine; Richard Orlinski for Daum, blue glass panther.

PAGES 86–87: Ettore Sottsass, totem; Hervé Van der Straeten, Lampadaire Electron 589; Venini, large dark blue vase; Clarita Brinkerhoff, *Albino Peacock*; Niki de Saint Phalle, *Nana* sculpture; Napoleone Martinuzzi, 21st Century Deco vase in aquamarine for Venini; Richard Ginori, porcelain urn; Carla Tolomeo, *Glazed Terracotta Figure of a Rhino with a Pelican*, 2012; Hervé Van der Straeten, Tabouret Capsule 215 in apple green.

PAGE 88: Vladimir Kagan, chair upholstered in a Josef Frank fabric from Schumacher; Gucci, pillow.

PAGE 89: Patrick Naggar, chaise longue upholstered in Nobilis's Velours Leopard; Renée Demsey (John's mother), needlepoint pillow; Haas Brothers, Flower lamp; Michael Eden, light blue 3D-printed resin urn.

PAGES 90–91: 1st row, second from left: Vikky Alexander, *Portage Glacier*, 1982; third from left: Daidō Moriyama, *Color*, 2016–17; right: Luke Gilford, *Lizzo*, 2019; 2nd row, left: Hiro, *The Light of Sikkim*, 1969; second from left: Hassan Hajjaj, *Cardi B*; third from left: Sylvie Blum, *Pop Lips III*, 2016; right: Horst P. Horst, *Susann Shaw*, 1943; 3rd row, left: Marilyn Minter, *Aquafresh*, 2020; Willy Rizzo, credenza; Georges Chevalier, Heritage Sun mirror; Zaha Hadid, second vase from right on mantel.

PAGES 92–93: Left: Alex Prager, *Jessica Joffe*; center: Miles Aldridge, *Pop Wife #3*, 2007; right: Francesco Scavullo, *Gloria Vanderbilt*, 1968; Baccarat, blue Eye vase; Viktor Schreckengost, blue ceramic bull; Guive Khosravi, *Le Nouveau Monde* vase; Christofle, silver panther.

PAGES 94–95: David Bass, horned animal head.

PAGE 96: Barware from Baccarat, Venini, and Steuben; decorative bust painted Yves Klein blue to match interior of barware cabinet; Kelly Wearstler, end table.

PAGE 96A: Wouter Hoste, ceramic column with a bronze glaze; Harvey Bouterse, ceramic face vase; Haas Brothers, Flower lamp; Muriel Rudolph (mother-in-law of Minnie Riperton, grandmother of Maya Rudolph), bronze lion head; Marcel Wanders for Baccarat, New Antique vase in amber.

PAGE 96B: Morgan Persson, vase.

FACES GATEFOLD OPENER: Left: Jaime Hayon, green glass vase; center: Hugh Findletar, Flowerheadz vase.

FACES GATEFOLD: Top row, fourth from left: Jonathan Baldock, *Maske XCVII*, 2022; Bottom row, far right: Jonathan Baldock, *Maske LXI*, 2020.

BACK OF FACES GATEFOLD–PAGE 97: Bar. Asprey, clear, blue, and amber crystal decanters with ram, fox, duck, and stag stoppers.

PAGES 98–99: Ruan Hoffmann, plates; David Bailey, prints from *Box of Pin-Ups*, 1965, from left: *John Lennon and Paul McCartney, Chrissie Shrimpton, Michael Caine, Jean Shrimpton, Mick Jagger and Max Maxwell*.

PAGES 100–101: Selection of Ruan Hoffmann plates.

PAGES 102–3: View from living room into library. David Bailey, prints from *Box of Pin-Ups*, 1965, last four on right: *Susan Murray, Lord Snowden, Cecil Beaton and Rudolf Nureyev, Michael Cooper*.

FLOOR TWO: LIBRARY

PAGES 104–5: Farrow & Ball, Rectory Red wall color; Charles Paris, Bubbles chandelier; David Hicks carpet pattern, reproduced by Stark; Christian Liaigre, couch; Guy de Rougemont, tripartite Golden Clover Coffee Table; Daum, Tropical Voyage Magnum vase (on coffee table); Gio Ponti, painting in window; Salvador Dalí, decorative object, third shelf from top on right; Alessandro Albrizzi, yellow desk; Jean-No, Silverback Gorilla for Daum.

PAGES 106–7: Steven Klein: blue *Nicki Minaj* for *Vogue*; Laurence Calabuig, *Diana Vreeland*.

PAGE 108: Geoffrey Bradfield, Lucite chair with yellow Ultrasuede; BDDW, wingback chair covered in a striped velour from Stark; La DoubleJ, pillow; Red Grooms, *Galactic Orbs (Yayoi Kusama)*, 2013 (behind the wingback chair).

PAGE 109: Laurie Hogin, *Love and Poison Monkey with Lipstick*, 2012; Pierre Frey, Utopia curtain fabric.

PAGES 110–11: Vintage Murano-glass fish; Jeff Zimmerman, organically shaped glass object; Judith Leiber, lion clutch; Hugh Findletar, Patook owl; Herend, mountain lion; vintage LeCoultre Atmos bronze clock; Kelly Wearstler, Bauble vase.

PAGE 112: Top right: Alessandro Mendini, Giotto vase for Venini; bird from Bergdorf Goodman's Christmas windows, 2021; bottom left: Jean Clemmer, *Hommage à Mae West: Mise-en-scène Figures*, 1967.

PAGE 113: DDG Frameshop, red-lacquered mirror.

PAGES 114–15: Fornasetti, plates for Louis Vuitton; Mia Fonssagrives-Solow, robot; L'Objet Haas Brothers, pair of *Lynda Boxes*; Madeleine van der Knoop, peacock for Daum; Wouter Hoste, abstract sculpture with glasses.

PAGE 116: Eric Schmitt, Chauffeuse Shell chair; Renée Demsey, needlepoint pillow; Pierre Yovanovitch, lip-shaped pillow.

PAGE 117: From top to bottom, three works by Kwame Brathwaite: *Untitled (Model Who Embraced Natural Hairstyles at Ajass Photoshoot)*, 1970; *Untitled (Black Is Beautiful Poster from 1970)*, 1970; *Changing Times*, 1973.

PAGES 118-19: Richard Bernstein, portrait of Diana Ross for the cover of the October 1981 issue of *Interview*; Sarah Faux, *Blush*, 2019 (painting above door); Willy Rizzo, *Elsa Martinelli*, 1967; Lalique, Baccarat, and Daum, animal figurines on shelf above door; Nymphenburg, owl to the left of photo of Elsa Martinelli; Ettore Sottsass, glass vases on far table.

PAGE 120: Top shelf: Baccarat, jungle cats; L'Objet Haas Brothers, *Lynda Box*; Joey Jalleo: photo of John with several of his dogs; bottom shelf: Véronique Rivemale, green-and-red vase; Oscar-like statue of Terry Richardson; leaded-glass statue of Lenin from Poland.

PAGE 121: Jimmie Martin, painted papier-mâché dog, sourced from Maison 24; Venini, large vase with white bands.

PAGE 122: Ruan Hoffmann, plate.

PAGE 123: Michael Eden, yellow 3D-printed resin urn; Hervé Van der Straeten, Lampe Pastilles.

PAGES 124–25: Top row, from left to right: Juergen Teller, *Stephanie Seymour*; Matthew Rolston, *Cyndi Lauper, Headdress, New York*, 1986; Harland Miller, *Armageddon*, 2017; Mario Testino, fashion photo for *Vogue*; Steven Klein, photo of Andy Warhol's portrait of Xiao Wen Ju as Marilyn Monroe for the cover of *Vogue Italia*'s China issue, June 2015; center row: Jonathan Becker, *Andy Warhol and His Corsets at the Fourth Factory, NY*, 1986; Miles Aldridge, *Donatella Versace*, 2007; bottom row: Bert Stern, *Elizabeth Taylor as Cleopatra*, 1962; Gucci, Pierre Yovanovitch, Renée Demsey, and Beatrice Mishel, pillows; Hermès and Gucci, throws.

PAGE 126: Powder room off library. Renée Demsey, painting of lady in red; Karl Springer, bench; Mia Fonssagrives-Solow, robot; Rafael Barrios, sculpture on vanity.

PAGE 127: Donald Robertson, illustrations; Campana Brothers, Miraggio mirror for Edra; Orrefors, vintage chandelier; Mia Fonssagrives-Solow, robot.

PAGE 128: Second-floor landing. 2nd row, right: David Bailey, *Mick Jagger*; 3rd row, left: Richard Phillips, signed reproduction of *Spectrum*, 1998; 4th row, left: Ron Galella, *Windblown Jackie*, 1971; 4th row, right: Guy Bourdin, fashion photo for French *Vogue*, 1966.

PAGE 129: Powder room between second and third floors. Willy Rizzo, mirror, 1970s; Donald Robertson, custom Dita Von Teese wallpaper and framed plate; Wayne Maser, photo of Dita von Teese; Elliott Erwitt, *Untitled, Chicago*, 1962; Ellen von Unwerth, *Playboy Bunnies*, New York, 1995.

FLOOR THREE

PAGE 132: Third-floor landing. Top row, left: Miles Aldridge, *Short Breaths #6*, 2012; top row, right: Miles Aldridge, *L'Ange Noir #1*, 2005; bottom row: Melvin Sokolsky, *Look Down, New York*, 1960.

PAGE 133: Top row, left: Harry Benson, *Valentino in Limo*, 1984; center row, center: Michael Avedon, *John Demsey*, 2020; center row, right: Davis Factor, *Morgan Freeman*, 1997; bottom row, center: Yousuf Karsh, *John Demsey*, 1975; bottom row, right: Ray Charles White, *David Hockney*, ca. 1987.

134-35: Angelo, master tailor of Zegna Bespoke Atelier, Milan, hand-drawn muslin jacket form.

PAGES 136-37: John Demsey's office. Jean Cocteau, plate; Donald Robertson, *Hermés Gas Station in Texas*; Lucien Clergue, *Pablo Picasso with a Cigarette, Cannes*, 1956; Daniele Fortuna, Yves Klein–blue bust; Bruno Gambone, ceramic bull; Hervé Van der Straeten, gold stack lamp; Gabriella Crespi, red Sedia Jacaré chair.

PAGE 138: Top row, left: Douglas Kirkland, *Betty Saint (Catroux) in Chanel's Pleated Sheer Cocktail Dress*, 1962; bottom row, right: William Klein, *Simone et Marines, Pont Alexandre III, Paris*, 1960; bust, sourced from Maison Gerard, vintage model of Eiffel Tower for Ralph Lauren Home; Louis Vuitton, model rocket ship; Pierre Frey, Kubus Argent window shade.

PAGE 139: Top row, right: William Klein, *Dorothy and Formfit, Paris*, 1960; center row, left: Lisa Eisner, surrealist face; center row, center: Arthur Elgort, *Kate Moss at Café Lipp, Paris, Vogue Italia*, 1993; center row, right: Niki de Saint Phalle, *La Danse (Hommage à Matisse)*, 1995; bottom row, right: William Klein, *Smoke + Veil (Vogue)*, 1958; Guy de Rougemont, Pop (Blue) lamp; Pedro Friedeberg, Hand Foot chair.

PAGES 140–41: Selection of Ruan Hoffmann plates.

PAGE 142: Bust, sourced at Marché aux Puces, Paris; Charles Lutz, *Debased Brillo*, based on Louis Vuitton trunks and Andy Warhol sculpture; Fornasetti, drawings lining base of wall; David Hicks carpet pattern, reproduced by Stark.

PAGE 143: Schumacher, La Cité wallpaper; Ruan Hoffmann, French-language plates; top left: Adam Kremer, photo of Nane Feist in Marc Jacobs's feather dress, for *New York* magazine, 2019; bottom left: Ruben Toledo, *Isabel Toledo*, 2012; top right: Pedro Friedeberg, Op Art work, 2011; Atelier Van Lieshout, Domestikator lamp.

PAGE 144: John Demsey's bedroom. Cynthia Daignault, *Monochrome Camaro*, 2022; Hugh Findletar, Flowerheadz vase; Guy de Rougemont, Pop (Red) lamp; André Joyau Studio, custom red-lacquered dresser.

PAGE 145: Le Manach, custom Leopard pillow; Hermès, tiger throw; Cloud bedside table in brass, sourced from JF Chen, Los Angeles; Hermès, black-lacquered horse head; Gabriella Crespi, lamp; mirrored lion head from Bergdorf Goodman's Christmas windows, 2018; Fornasetti, cube; Grisha Bruskin, *Male Beast*.

PAGES 146–47: Benjamin Moore, Caliente wall color; Pierre Frey, Emilio Gold window shades; Apparatus Studio: ceiling fixture; Len Prince, lips photos; Elizabeth Garouste, bronze Look mirror; Bibi Monnahan for Houston Upholstery, headboard in Schumacher's Tiger pattern; D. Porthault, Bois de Moiré linens; Richard Orlinski, gorilla sculpture; top right: Mark Gagnon, *All Glam Monkey*, portrait of John Demsey as a monkey in a Thom Browne suit; bottom right: Miles Aldridge, *Lip Sync #3*, 2001; bench, sourced from Antony Todd; David Hicks carpet pattern, reproduced by Stark.

PAGE 148: Gabriella Crespi, lamp; Jane Black, watercolor of bedroom; Robert Goossens, bronze cat with the face of Loulou de La Falaise, from the collection of Loulou de La Falaise.

PAGE 149: Details of John's bedroom.

PAGE 150: Top shelf: Nymphenburg, white monkey; Fornasetti, red vase; bottom shelf: Jaime Hayon, Strypy Special Edition Bosa Vase; Michael Geertsen, red-and-gold abstract sculpture.

PAGE 151: Vintage Pierre Cardin, circular lamp on windowsill; Joe Colombo, Elda lounge chair, 1960s; Lotus Arts de Vivre, red leather Bulldog stool; Fornasetti, magazine rack.

PAGES 152–53: Dressing room. Shirts by Charvet, Berluti, Wil Whiting; fragrances by Tom Ford Private Blend, and Frédéric Malle; sunglasses by Morgenthal Frederics, Cartier, Tom Ford, and Jacques Marie Mage.

PAGES 154–55: Christophe von Hohenberg, *Fashion Designer Halston with Liza Minnelli* (attending Andy Warhol's memorial service), 1987; Tory Burch, pillow.

PAGE 156: Shoes by John Lobb, Berluti, and J.M. Weston; custom velvet slippers by Gaziano & Girling.

PAGE 157: Cashmere and wool socks by Charvet, Thom Browne, Berluti, and Loro Piana.

PAGES 158–59: Pocket squares by Charvet, Hermès, Zegna, Anderson & Sheppard, and Turnbull & Asser.

PAGE 160: Emily Rand, drawing of John for Taillour tailoring studios, London.

PAGE 160A: Wooden torso, sourced at Marché aux Puces, Paris; vintage male figurine.

PAGE 160B: Zegna XXX jacket with custom-patterned silk lining.

JACKET LININGS GATEFOLD OPENER: Emily Rand, drawing of John for Taillour tailoring studios, London.

JACKET LININGS GATEFOLD: Zegna XXX bespoke leather, suede, and cashmere jackets with custom-patterned linings.

BACK OF JACKET LININGS GATEFOLD–PAGE 161: Leather and suede jackets by Hermès, Tom Ford, Bottega Veneta, Zegna, Michael Browne, Céline, and Loro Piana.

FLOOR FOUR

PAGES 164–65: Left: Terry Richardson, photos of lips; top right: Adam Kremer, *Elizabeth Davison, Metal Curls (Vogue China)*, 2019; bottom right: Guy Bourdin, photo for *French Vogue*, 1971

PAGES 166–67: Miles Aldridge, *Actress #6*, 2012.

PAGES 168–69: Guest bedroom. Kelly Wearstler, Chalet wallpaper; D. Porthault: Pois de Senteur linens; Louise Mishel (John's great-aunt, twin of his maternal grandfather), painting of girl in a striped dress; Renée Demsey, all other paintings; assorted vintage vases; David Hicks carpet pattern, reproduced by Stark.

PAGE 170: Gio Ponti, desk; Gucci Décor, Chiavari chair with embroidered tiger; Fornasetti, magazine rack.

PAGE 171: Vintage slipper chair upholstered in a Madeline Weinrib ikat fabric.

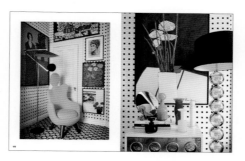

PAGES 172: Vincent Darré, Conversation chair.

PAGE 173: Vintage Murano-glass vases; Hervé Van der Straeten, mirror.

PAGE 174: Sylvie Blum, *Candy Lips I*, 2014.

PAGE 175: Guest bathroom. Donald Robertson, prints; Miles Aldridge, *Actress #6*, 2012; D. Porthault, Coquelicots Parisiens towels.

PAGES 176–77: Guest bedroom. Kelly Wearstler, Coquette wallpaper; D. Porthault, Pois de Senteur linens; André Joyau Studio, black-lacquered side table; Fornasetti, lamp.

PAGES 178–79: Renée Demsey, paintings; vintage Scandinavian monkey figurine on windowsill; Adrienne Rogers, red blanket; Christian Liaigre, chair on left, upholstered in Dinosauria by House of Hackney; Gerrit Rietveld, Utrecht armchair for Cassina, upholstered in Bertjan Pot Boxblocks.

PAGE 180: Renée Demsey, painting.

PAGE 181: Renée Demsey, paintings; André Joyau Studio, green-lacquered dresser; Loewe Weaves, pompom vase; Kenneth Snelson, aluminum-and-wire sculpture.

PAGES 182–83: Marie Helene Demsey's bedroom. Schumacher, Blommen wallpaper and headboard fabric; Bibi Monnahan, headboard design; Alber Elbaz, doll and painted mirror for Lanvin; Renée Demsey, left and right needlepoint pillows; Beatrice Mishel, center needlepoint pillow; Jaime Hayon, Candy Light table lamp for Baccarat; Bottega Veneta, floor lamp with custom textile shade by Celine Cannon.

PAGES 184–85: André Joyau Studio, desk; vintage mirror from the estate of John's maternal great-grandmother, Masha Mishel; Lanvin, fashion figurines; Elena Cutolo, Canopie series ceramic vessel; Bruno Gambone, ceramic cow; small carrying case covered in Voutsa Everyday Lips wallpaper.

PAGE 186: Top row: Maurizio Cattelan and Pierpaolo Ferrari, Shit vase; Elena Cutolo, Canopie series ceramic vessels; center row: Lanvin, figurines; bottom row: Bruno Gambone, stoneware animal figurines.

PAGE 187: Marie Helene Demsey, dressed in LoveShackFancy and Dior sneakers; robot from Bergdorf Goodman Christmas windows, 2021.

PAGE 188: Marie Helene Demsey's bathroom. Black Edition, Kew wallpaper in Jaipur Pink for ROMO; D. Porthault, towels; Turnbull & Asser, silk foulards depicting John's dogs Scout (top) and Naomi (bottom); Terry O'Neill, *Audrey Hepburn Dove*, 1967; Irving Haberman, Marilyn Monroe during an interview with Edward R. Murrow on *Person to Person*, ca. 1955.

PAGE 189: Terry O'Neill, Audrey Hepburn (top three photos); photo of Marlo Thomas as Ann Marie in *That Girl*; Ruben Toledo, fashion illustration; Louise Michel, portrait of a woman.

FLOOR FIVE

PAGE 192: The "Factory" sitting room. Top left: Warhol-inspired soup can, given to John by his godfather in honor of John's nickname for Marie Helene, "Sweet Pea"; top right: Alex Katz, silk screen; bottom left: Abidiel Vicente & Houssein Jarouche, *Astronaut Monochromie—Radar (green)*; bottom right: Miles Aldridge, A *Drop of Red #2*, 2001; Soane Britain, red leather chair; Gucci, pillow; Victor Douieb, *Pop Art Rhino*, 2015.

PAGES 194–95: Miles Aldridge, *Ex Libris*, 2019.

PAGE 196: Miles Aldridge, *Extravagant Sophisticated Lady #12*, 2011.

PAGE 197: Vintage Serge Mouille ceiling fixture; Ray Charles White, *Front Surface Reflection*; mirrored horse head from Bergdorf Goodman Christmas windows, 2017.

PAGES 198–99: Top left: Sylvie Blum, *Swimcap*, 2016; bottom left: Miles Aldridge, *Cat Story #3*, 2008; John Isaacs, *The Architecture of Empathy* (neon tubing, reading "tears welling up inside"), 2014; Ray Charles White, *Surface Tension*; center right: Sara Greenberger Rafferty, *Positive*, 2018; bottom right: André de Dienes, *In a Swimming Pool, Hollywood*, 1950s.

PAGES 200–201: Center: Anne Collier, *Woman Crying #13*, 2017; left and right: Monique Baumann, collages; B&B Italia, red velvet couch; David Schaefer, red- and white-lacquered tables; Rianna + Nina, peacock pillows; Gucci, center pillow; Michael Geertsen, abstract sculpture on floor; Kelly Wearstler, limited-edition *Head Trip* sculpture; Willy Rizzo, tortoiseshell pyramid; Fornasetti, Smilzo Charlot Black/White vase.

PAGES 202-3: Edra, mirrored cabinet; Andrew Unangst, *Andy Warhol with Red Campbell's Soup*, 1985; Ruan Hoffmann, plates; Vincent Darré, vase on floor.

PAGES 204-5: Fornasetti, geometrically patterned plates; Christian Liaigre, desk; India Mahdavi, pink Charlotte chair; Pucci, pillow; Fornasetti, stool; Curtis Jeré, *Sputnik* sculpture.

PAGES 206-7: Jayde Cardinalli, print depicting the Demsey animal kingdom; Dan McCarthy, smiling face vase; Lladró, ceramic tiger; Hugh Findletar, red-lipped face mask; Willy Rizzo, chrome lamp.

PAGE 208: Miles Aldridge, *Extravagant Sophisticated Lady #12*, 2011; Fornasetti, blue face vase; Hugh Findletar, lion mask.

PAGE 209: Bird from Bergdorf Goodman Christmas windows, 2022. Missoni carpet pattern for Stark; vintage seal sculpture; Robert Lazzarini, paintings on right.

PAGES 210-11: David Schaefer, cast-iron bookcase; top: Nymphenburg, raven; Michael Geertsen, red-and-yellow sculpture; 1st shelf: Venini, banded vases; Michael Graves for Tiffany, silver vase; 2nd shelf: Ruan Hoffmann, monkey sculpture; 4th shelf: Flair, white bisque horse; vintage Italian red floor lamp.

PAGES 212-13: Fortuny, Studio 76 Tripod floor lamp, black and gold leaf; Tony Kelly, photo of RuPaul for cover of *Plastik* magazine, no. 35, 2019.

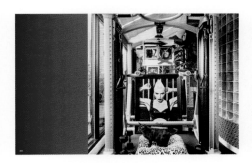

PAGES 214-15: Gym. William Klein, *Muhammad Ali, Miami*, 2019, c-print from unique painted contact; Steven Klein, photo of Daphne Guinness, 2016.

PAGES 216-17: Custom CYBEX Technogym and Hoist equipment; Shepard Fairey, *Sedation Pill*, 2014; Scott King, *Cher Guevara*, 2008; Studio Job & Seletti, Mouth Neon Lamp; Charles P. Mills and Lee Boultin, Twiggy in Pierre Cardin's asymmetrical sunglasses, 1967.

PAGES 218-19: Fifth-floor bathroom. Eileen Gray, mirror; Gregory Johnston, metal disks.

Behind the Blue Door: A Maximalist Mantra
First published in 2023 by The Vendome Press
Vendome is a registered trademark of The Vendome Press LLC

VENDOME PRESS US
P.O. Box 566
Palm Beach, FL 33480

VENDOME PRESS UK
Worlds End Studio
132–134 Lots Road
London, SW10 0RJ

www.vendomepress.com

Distributed in North America by Abrams Books
Distributed in the United Kingdom, and the rest of the world, by Thames & Hudson

ISBN 978-0-86565-434-1

Publishers: Beatrice Vincenzini, Mark Magowan, and Francesco Venturi
Editor: Jacqueline Decter
Production Director: Jim Spivey
Designer: Rita Sowins / Sowins Design

Library of Congress Cataloging-in-Publication Data
available upon request

Printed and bound in China by RR Donnelley (Guangdong) Printing Solutions Company Ltd.

First printing

PHOTO CREDITS: All photographs by Douglas Friedman, with the exception of the following:
Ethan Herrington: pp. 1, 14–15, 48B, Animals gatefold, 96B, Faces gatefold, 158–59, 160, 160B,
     Jacket Linings gatefold opener, Jacket Linings gatefold
Connor Brothers: p. 16
Miles Aldridge: pp. 22–23, 64, 77, 166–67, 194–95, 196, 198–99 bottom left
Ben Hassett: pp. 36–37 top and bottom right
David LaChapelle: p. 67
Sylvie Blum: pp. 174, 198–99 top left

PAGE 1: John Demsey's custom monogram, created by Berluti's Arnys bespoke tailoring workshop.
PAGES 220-21: John Demsey, dressed in custom Zegna; dogs, from left to right: Roxy, Gizmo, Biscuit, Zeus, Sugar, Bella, and Diego; Andy Warhol x Gufram, *Andy's Blue Cactus*; Sui Jianguo, resin dinosaur; column painted Yves Klein blue, sourced from 1stDibs; Christopher Maschinot, ceramic face vase; Hervé Van der Straeten, small planter at foot of column; monkey sculpture, sourced from Blackman Cruz; Patrick Naggar, Amalfi outdoor chairs; Knoll, benches.